A Mother's Search for Santa

BY

Dawn Nolan

iUniverse, Inc.
New York   Bloomington

iUniverse books may be ordered through booksellers or by contacting:

iUniverse
1663 Liberty Drive
Bloomington, IN 47403
www.iuniverse.com
1-800-Authors (1-800-288-4677)

Because of the dynamic nature of the Internet, any Web addresses or links contained in this book may have changed since publication and may no longer be valid. The views expressed in this work are solely those of the author and do not necessarily reflect the views of the publisher, and the publisher hereby disclaims any responsibility for them.

ISBN: 978-1-4401-3531-6 (sc)
ISBN: 978-1-4401-3533-0 (ebook)

Library of Congress Control Number: 2009930728

Printed in the United States of America

iUniverse rev. date: 7/3/2009

To all of my beautiful grandsons and to my daughter who asked the question.

Acknowledgments

Thank you to my husband and my friend Amy for the help with the illustrations. I give a special thank-you to my spiritual friend, Monika, who supplied me with some tools for my quest. Most of all, I'd like to give thanks to the Lord for guiding me on my search for the answer I needed.

It was a beautiful fall day: the trees were just beginning to drop their leaves. Lynn loved to sit by the window and watch her boys, Sam, who was six, Andrew, who was eight, and their friend Christopher, who was nine and lived next door, use their imaginations playing games they made up and games she had passed down to them from her childhood. She didn't want them sitting in the house playing video games and watching too much television.

Suddenly, Sam threw open the front door and ran into the house. Lynn turned around and was surprised to see him looking very upset.

Lynn had seen the three boys standing by the tree and talking, looking very serious. Maybe they were making the rules for the next game of tag or the password for the club they had just formed, which had only three members as of yesterday.

Lynn extended her arms to her youngest son as he anxiously approached her.

"What happened? Why are you so upset?" she asked, drawing him into her arms for comfort.

Sam frowned at his mother and took a deep breath before speaking. "Mom, Christopher said that Santa is made up, just to make kids behave for their parents or else they won't get any toys. He said Santa is just a lie!"

Lynn knew that any time now her boys would learn of the reality of the whole Santa Claus thing, but she had hoped there would be another season left for that fun-filled magic of make-believe. With the boys being so close, she supposed they would learn most things together from here on out. With a sigh and a brush of her hand through his hair, she said, "Sam, it's okay. We'll talk about this later. For now, I want you to go tell your brother to come inside to get cleaned up and you both can help me get ready for dinner."

That evening, Lynn tucked her boys into bed. She told them not to worry about what Christopher had said, yet she didn't deny his words. She knew they would bring this subject up again soon, and she needed to be ready. After a kiss good night, Lynn slipped from their room and went right to the phone to call me. With concern in her voice, she said, "Mom, I have a question I need your help with. What does Santa have to do with Christmas?"

Wow, I was stumped! It's not that I hadn't pondered the thought before, but I'd never had to come up with an answer. I asked, "Lynn, where is this coming from?"

"Mom, the kids were outside playing with Christopher, and he told them that Santa was just a lie. Sam was so upset, and Andrew is waiting for me to tell them Santa is real. I'm just not sure I can or should even try to prove Christopher wrong," she said with anxiety in her voice. I told my daughter I'd get back to her on it before the holidays. I felt that this was one of the most important answers I might ever need to come up with. I wasn't really sure why I felt that way.

As the days went by, I had to ask myself if Santa should even be in the mix of Christmas symbols. I looked at the commercial aspect of it first. Over the past few years, I had felt as though people didn't seem to remember Christ at Christmas anymore.

I actually started to become a little depressed. I loved Christmas and Santa and everything that went along with the holiday season. I turned to prayer. I asked the Lord the question, "What does Santa have to do with it? Is believing in Santa okay?"

After several days, I started getting my answers. I was doing dishes at the kitchen sink when all of a sudden, it hit me. I turned from the sink and just stared out the kitchen window in thought.

"I know now what I can tell my daughter." It's the beginning of faith. It's the beginning of learning what faith is. It's a child's way of learning to believe. "Wow!" I said, "Is that it, Lord? Is that what Santa has to do with Christmas?" I wanted to ponder this thought a while before going back to my daughter with this answer.

So many things began to unfold. I didn't want to think we should discourage the idea of Santa. I needed to be open to hear the answer, not only for my daughter and grandchildren, but also for myself. This became a real spiritual search.

Each morning, I started my day with coffee and read a daily devotional that was given to me by my good friend. It always gave me a subject to discuss with the Lord before work. This was a half-a-pot morning. I had a big discussion ahead of me. I needed to know if I was on the right track. I picked up the page that had been given to me the day before; the title read, "Blessed are those who believe without seeing."

The thoughts in the devotional for the day were about receiving knowledge and being responsible to pass it on to others. They were about walking in the footsteps of those who had gone before.

The message was becoming clear. I decided to test this first on my husband, who often critiques my good ideas and my not-so-good ideas. We sat down with a peaceful cup of coffee. After I explained what I had been struggling with, he patiently listened to the answer I wanted to present.

I began, "Oh, yes, I sure do believe in Santa. But that isn't really his name, and he doesn't really have a long beard. Well, at least I don't think he does. I really doubt he wears a red suit. I'm positive he is not fat or an elf. He doesn't have a workshop at the North Pole. He doesn't ride on a sleigh pulled by his reindeer, delivering toys to children all over the world by squeezing down the chimney with a ho-ho-ho. This is all just a fun image we use for children. He does see you when you're sleeping, and he knows when you're awake. He knows if you are bad or good. Get the picture?"

"You cannot be saying what I think you're saying." My husband looked at me as if I had lost my marbles.

I continued, "All I'm trying to say is the spirit of Christmas and Santa show the children how to believe in someone they can't really see in action. It's someone who can see you always, any time and any place. He comes in miraculously and bestows gifts on them. I just feel telling children about Santa is not lying; it's just pretending. Children's beliefs transition from a dream and wish into a prayer to the Lord and faith that he'll hear." I reminded my husband that the history of Santa shows us that Santa has been evolving since his beginning.

I asked my husband to just sit and reflect on when he was a child and when he thought of Santa.

"Remember the feeling of excitement in writing a letter, listing the things you wanted, and the nights lying in bed, wondering if they would be brought to you? Or going to kindergarten wearing the new outfit you never even asked for but were so happy Santa gave to you? You might not have gotten *everything* you asked for, but when you did receive your gifts, you pretty much forgot what you didn't get. You just enjoyed what you *did* receive."

As adults, we pray to the Lord for things, whether it is finances, health, or love, and hope he will hear us; whatever we pray for, we wait and hope he will give to us. We're not little children. We know we won't receive everything we ever ask for, and we know there are reasons, even if we can't understand them right then.

How many adults remember when Santa didn't bring them a horse to live in their backyard? I never got mine. I guess Santa had his reasons for not giving me that horse. I still laugh at that, because I really am not a horse person—although as a teen I did try to be. Oh, the aches and pains of that! Whenever I think about the visits to friends that had horses and all the falls, I think of all the times I hoped Santa would bring me a horse and didn't. Thank the Lord for that!

What about the "love of your life," the one you didn't get to marry? You go to a class reunion and thank the Lord for your spouse. There are a lot of things I am so thankful for not receiving. Whether I was asking Santa as a young child or praying as a worldly, mature teen, I'm sure glad the Lord cared enough to give me what I needed rather than what I wanted.

Now, we all grew up hearing, "If you don't behave, Santa won't bring you anything." I needed to pray about this because we have all known children that misbehave excessively yet still receive more than they seem to deserve.

The answer came very easily the next morning. Don't we do the same with God? It's often easy to wonder why somebody who sins so boldly seems to receive so much. What about the person sitting in prison for a horrible crime who claims to have been reborn? I have to remind myself that the Lord is the only one that can judge the hearts of man.

Therefore, to be consistent, Santa would know if a child was trying to behave better. I would make sure to discuss this with my daughter. I would also tell her that as it is hard to not give our children something that they might really want, so are the consequences of wrong behavior. Right now we are just talking about Santa, but shouldn't we really be teaching self-restraint from sin? The Lord lets us make decisions, but he does not reward us for sin. With this answer, to my surprise, I thought all the dots were connecting.

I suggested to my husband that we plan a movie night and stay up late to watch Christmas movies. He wasn't all that surprised because he knows I have always shopped year-round with Christmas in mind. It was only late October, yet I was ready to put my tree up. The following weekend, I went out and rented several movies, starting with *It's a Wonderful Life*. This movie stars Jimmy Stewart—what a great classic movie!

We put the popcorn bowl out, and when the movie was over, we talked about what we thought the meaning was and what we got out of it. Santa wasn't in this movie. It was the holiday season, the Christmas tree was up, and snow was on the ground. The movie simply makes you think of the little things a person might do to affect the lives of others not only during the holiday season but all year and always. It wasn't a religious movie at all, or at least it didn't seem to be. I'd seen this movie at least thirty times in my life, yet each time I see it I am reminded that a kind word or a helpful hand may be what will make someone's life better, in a small way or in a big way. This movie shows how important it is that we live, no matter how unimportant we feel we are at times. It doesn't even sound like a holiday movie, but it is played every winter and is a favorite during the holiday season.

The next evening we put in *Miracle on 34th Street.* Now we're talking—a movie about Santa. This classic movie was about a divorced woman with a child. She raised her child to not believe in make-believe. No Santa, fairy tales, or any other kind of pretending. The woman was portrayed as being bitter and distrusting. Her faith had been shaken.

It was also about a nice old man that believed he was Santa, and a handsome bachelor who wanted it all. Of course, in the end, the miracle did happen. And of course it was more than a present from Santa under a Christmas tree. Yet the movie was portrayed in a way that felt like Santa could perform miracles. The message was spelled out in the title. We all know where miracles come from. I really have never heard anyone tell their child Santa can bring you a miracle. I'm not trying to stretch a child's imagination that far, either.

I really hadn't given that much thought to all the old classic Christmas movies; they were just that, Christmas movies. But now I was watching them with a new way of thinking. I was searching for meaning. We talked about the movie *A Christmas Carol,* another movie that did not have Santa in it yet was definitely a Christmas movie. This one's message is to change your ways before it's too late. Ebenezer Scrooge is shown his past and his present and the gloom and doom of his future if he stays on the same path. This holds a lesson of giving instead of greed, and caring instead of bitterness. Gee, that message is pretty clear— and not just at Christmas.

At the end of our weekend holiday-movie fest, we spent the evening discussing different holiday movies and how they all seemed to hold a message to be practiced all year round. Late in the evening as we made our way to bed, my husband gave me a kiss and a wink and said, "I think your search for Santa is over."

Now that the presence of Santa and the magical feel of Christmas were far more clear, it was time to give the answer to my daughter. It was now the latter part of November, on a day our family came together to give thanks for our blessings and the time we have to share with each other.

We finished our meal, and I asked my daughter to come sit by the fire with me. I told her I was ready to answer her question about what I believed Santa had to do with it. I let her know that this answer was for her; I would not share it with her children but with my own child. She would know what to do with it and when.

I took a deep swallow, sent a silent prayer for the right words, and began.

Children around the world go to bed on Christmas Eve, and before they fall asleep, they wish and hope for a man in a red suit to come down the chimney and bring them something special that they want so much. Like *the candy cane*, Santa's suit is red and white. White symbolizes the purity of Jesus's birth, and the red symbolizes the blood shed by Christ on the cross so that we could have our sins forgiven and have eternal life. The Lord brings blessings to some we may not believe deserve them, but this is not for us to judge, the same way a child may see a friend or sibling receive something from Santa even if the child didn't always mind his or her parents.

It's fun to watch children use their imaginations. It's fun to watch them pretend they are a cowboy or an elephant. Believing in Santa, a very nice fat man in a suit, lasts only for a short time, as it should be. It grows and changes from mailing Santa a letter to sending a prayer to heaven. It grows from jumping up and down and saying, "Look what Santa brought me!" to saying a prayer of thanks. Instead of thanking Santa, children begin to thank their parents, and their parents thank the Lord that they were fortunate enough to afford to give those gifts at Christmas.

Instead of wondering what Santa will bring, which they eventually learn comes from their parents, children transition into prayer. With that transition comes the knowledge that Christmas is a time of giving and kindness, not just receiving. I think seeing the lights on the houses, the decorated Christmas trees, and the Santa costumes and being filled with happy cheer of magical times brings your attention back to the knowledge that anything is possible because Christmas is all about Christ.

I do believe in Santa, because I believe that children should be able to dream and hope as large as they want to. Then as they grow, they will pray just as earnestly, with the faith that they may not receive everything they ask for but will always receive everything they need. They will know anything is possible.

Now when I think of Santa, my heart fills with a warm happiness, and I am reminded to say a prayer of thanks for my blessings and for the children in my life.

Lynn sat quietly for a moment, and with tears in her eyes, my daughter gave me a heartfelt hug and thanked me for my answer. Before going home that night, she told me she was no longer dreading when her boys would understand where the gifts under the Christmas tree came from.

The days turned into weeks, and before I knew it, it was Christmas. My husband and I arrived at my daughter's family home Christmas morning. Lynn shared with me how her Christmas Eve went. She said that at bedtime she had explained to the boys about Santa and what we had talked about.

Lynn said she wasn't really sure what they thought until they were opening their gifts this morning, when Sam looked at his parents and said, "Hey! Look what God let you get me!" They all laughed, and Lynn knew that Santa could still visit their home.

Tonight it would not be Santa they would thank for their presents, and they no longer needed to wait for Christmas or look under the Christmas tree for their gifts. They had prayer year-round. Christ was put back into Christmas, and Santa still represented childhood fun and festivities and joy during the holidays.

As for me, that night, I curled up on the sofa next to my husband and sent up a prayer of thanks for my special coffee time and the best Christmas ever. As they say, Christmas is for kids, and we're all God's children.

That's What Santa Has to Do with It!

The End

This book was not written to change the way a person worships or what he or she believes. Yet I hope it may bring tolerance and understanding to the way some celebrate. Most important is that we all have the Lord in our lives to guide us to the answers we need.

Merry Christmas